Let's Explore Russia

by Walt K. Moon

BUMBA BOOKS™

LERNER PUBLICATIONS ◆ MINNEAPOLIS

Note to Educators:

Throughout this book, you'll find critical thinking questions. These can be used to engage young readers in thinking critically about the topic and in using the text and photos to do so.

Lerner Publications Company
A division of Lerner Publishing Group, Inc.
241 First Avenue North
Minneapolis, MN 55401 USA

For reading levels and more information, look up this title at www.lernerbooks.com.

Library of Congress Cataloging-in-Publication Data

Names: Moon, Walt K., author.
Title: Let's explore Russia / by Walt K. Moon.
Description: Minneapolis : Lerner Publications, [2017] | Includes bibliographical references and index.
Identifiers: LCCN 2016018687 (print) | LCCN 2016022116 (ebook) | ISBN 9781512430097 (library bound : alkaline paper) | ISBN 9781512430110 (paperback : alkaline paper) | ISBN 9781512430127 (pb)
Subjects: LCSH: Russia (Federation)—Juvenile literature.
Classification: LCC DK510.23 .M66 2017 (print) | LCC DK510.23 (ebook) | DDC 947—dc23

LC record available at https://lccn.loc.gov/2016018687

Manufactured in the United States of America
1 – VP – 12/31/16

Expand learning beyond the printed book. Download free, complementary educational resources for this book from our website, www.lernerresource.com.

Table of Contents

A Visit to Russia

Russia is partly in Europe.

It is partly in Asia.

It is the biggest country.

Millions of people

live there.

Russia has cold areas.

These areas are called tundra.

Few trees grow in the tundra.

Why do you think few trees grow in the tundra?

Foxes live in the tundra.

Snowy owls fly in the sky.

Russia has large forests.

Many bears live in them.

Most big cities are in the west.

Moscow is the largest city.

Few people live in the east.

Lots of people travel to Russia.

They visit museums.

They see famous churches.

What do you think people see in museums?

Many Russian people eat borscht.

Borscht is a soup made from beets.

People also bake.

They make bread and cakes.

borscht

Games are popular
in Russia.

Many people play chess.

People also play bandy.

This sport is like
ice hockey.

**Why might
bandy be popular
in Russia?**

Russia is a beautiful country.

There are many things to see.

Would you like to visit Russia?

Map of Russia

tundra

oceans

Russia

forests

Moscow

Picture Glossary

borscht

a soup made from beets

chess

a popular two-player game that uses a board and moveable pieces

museums

places where art and objects from the past are on display

tundra

cold areas with frozen ground and few trees

23

Index

Read More

Kabakov, Vladimir. *R Is for Russia.* London: Frances Lincoln Children's Books, 2013.

King, Dedie. *I See the Sun in Russia.* Hardwick, MA: Satya House Publications, 2014.

York, M. J. *Learn Russian Words.* Mankato, MN: Child's World, 2015.

Photo Credits